SPEAK RIGHT UP
BEGINNER

Public Speaking Training
For Students in Grade Levels 1-12

Abe George
Founder of Young Speakers Club, Institute for Public Speaking and Communication Training

Speak Right Up Beginner

Public Speaking Training for Students in Grade Levels 1-12

by Abe George

Published by Geo Publishers, LLC
Fairfax, Virginia, U.S.A.
Email: geopublishers.usa@gmail.com

ISBN: 978-1-7332852-0-9

10 9 8 7 6 5 4 3 2 1

Cover Photo: Martin Luther King, Jr. Memorial, Washington, DC
Photo by: Abe George

Contents

Plan - Prepare - Practice - Perform

Image by David Mark from Pixabay

Introduction

This is a textbook and a workbook for students to improve their public speaking and communication skills. The lessons in this book are based on research in the field of education and psychology and the exercises are based on proven methods used in the Young Speakers Club classrooms over the last 15 years.

Beginner lessons in this book focus on helping students develop self-confidence and better public speaking style by building the habits of eye contact, posture and gestures, and voice modulation. Assignments and exercises help students overcome stage fright and present their ideas to the audience with clarity and impact. Other textbooks/workbooks in this series (Speak Right Up Intermediate, Advanced, and Master) focus on improving students' skills in writing speeches, researching the audience, pushing beyond the comfort zone, using humor and stories in their speeches, and practicing special topics such as debate and project presentations.

Educators agree that the essential skills students should gain for the 21st century are Communication, Critical Thinking, Creativity, and Collaboration - the four C's. The speech topics and the research questions will help students think critically and creatively. The class discussions on speech topics will improve their collaboration skills. Presenting the speeches in front of the class will help them overcome stage fright, improve presentation skills, and build better habits of communication. By making Speak Right Up training a regular weekly exercise for students, parents and teachers can help them become better communicators, better thinkers, and better leaders.

If you are interested in forming a Young Speakers Club in your school, church, or community, where students can meet weekly and work through the lessons and exercises to improve their public speaking skills, I will be glad to provide you with additional materials that you can use in the club. You may contact me at the email address given below.

Abe George
Fairfax, Virginia
YoungSpeakersClub@gmail.com

For Jessy, Jacob, and John

John George and Jacob George co-hosting the Graduation Ceremony of Young Speakers Club students.

Public Speaking

Why effective communication is an essential skill for the 21st century.

LESSON OBJECTIVES

- Understand what public speaking is.
- Understand the importance of public speaking.
- Learn to develop effective communication skills.
- Deliver your first speech.

Good communication skills are incredibly important and something that almost anybody can improve upon, both in writing and speaking. A relatively modest improvement can make a major difference in your future earning power, as well as in many other aspects of your life.

Warren Buffett

Photo by Rob Laughter

PRINCIPLES

1.1. Communication

Communication is the art of transferring information, meaning, and emotion between sender and receiver. Public Speaking is a special form of communication, where one person acts as the sender (the Speaker) and several others act simultaneously as receivers (the Audience).

According to research, effective communication skill is the most requested skill by employers for almost all leadership positions. Communication skills are also important for success in group projects and class participation in school and college.

Learning the principles of communication and practicing the techniques of public speaking will improve your effectiveness in studies, careers, and personal life. It will also improve your self-confidence and interpersonal skills.

Photo by Priscilla Du Preez

As a beginner in public speaking, it's better for you to stand in the center of the stage so that you have the audience distributed equally to your left and right sides.

If you hold the microphone in one hand, as shown in the photo, make sure to hold that hand steady while you use the other hand for gestures. If you leave the microphone on a stand or use a clip-on mic, you will be able to use both hands for hand gestures.

1.2. Public Speaking

What is public speaking? It is a form of communication where one person speaks to a group of listeners with a specific objective. Let's look at some of the characteristics of public speaking.

- There is one speaker.

- There are several listeners. They are called the audience.

- The speaker has an objective. Examples of some objectives are "inform the audience", "inspire the audience", or "entertain the audience".

- Most of the time, the speaker is standing up and facing the audience. This is the most uncomfortable part of public speaking for many people.

The skill of public speaking and communication is necessary to be successful in every field and profession.

Communication is effective when it stimulates meaning in another person's mind and successful when it influences another person for intended actions.

PUBLIC SPEAKING BEGINNER

SPEECH ASSIGNMENT

Grades 1-4

Speech Topic: **Self Introduction**

Speech Objective: **Introduce yourself and your school in an interesting way.**

INTRODUCTION

- Address the audience: **"Ladies and Gentlemen!"**
- Introduce the topic: **"Let me introduce myself and my school to you in the next few minutes."**

BODY

- Address the following questions:
  - What is your name?
  - Do you play any sports or do any arts?
- **"Now, I want to tell you about an interesting place where I go almost everyday. It is my school."**
- Give some details of your school:
  - What is the name of your school?
  - How big is it?
  - What are some of the things you like about your school?

CONCLUSION

- Conclude your speech by telling the audience what you want them to remember: **"Even if you don't remember most of the things that I just told you, I hope you will remember my name. It is _____."**
- **"Thank you."**

SPEECH ASSIGNMENT

Grades 5-12

Speech Topic: **Self Introduction**

Speech Objective: **Introduce yourself and your school in an interesting way.**

INTRODUCTION

- Address the audience: **"Ladies and Gentlemen!"**
- Introduce the topic: **"I would like to introduce to you myself and my school in the next few minutes."**

BODY

- Address the following questions:
  - What is your name?
  - What are your sports interests?
  - What are your hobbies?
  - Have you seen any interesting movies or read any interesting books recently?
- **"Now, I want to tell you about my school."**
- Address the following questions:
  - What is the name of your school?
  - How big is it?
  - What are some of the things you like about your school?
  - What are some of the things you dislike about your school?

CONCLUSION

- Conclude your speech by telling the audience what you want them to remember the most: **"Even if you don't remember anything that I just told you, please remember just one thing - my name. It is _____."**
- **"Thank you."**

A NEW WORD TO USE IN YOUR SPEECH

appease

Meaning: To make peaceful and quiet; to calm; to satisfy

Example: My science teacher always appease the nervous students before the test.

HOW TO PRESENT THE SPEECH

Enter the stage with a smile. It shows your confidence to the audience.

Keep eye contact with the audience. You are speaking to the audience, so that's where you should be looking at. You are not speaking to the floor or the back wall or the ceiling. So, when your eyes stray away to these places, bring it back to the audience.

Speak up. Audience should be able to hear you clearly.

SPEECH OUTLINE

Speech Title:

Through Line: Write the main idea of your speech in one or two sentences.

Introduction: Present your topic in an interesting way to hook the audience.

Body - Point 1: The idea, data, and examples.

Body - Point 2: The idea, data, and examples.

Conclusion: The main point that you want your audience to remember.

QUESTIONS AND EXERCISES

1   What is communication?

2   What is public speaking? What are some of the characteristics of public speaking?

3   Think about a topic that you talked with your friends. It may be about a class, a movie, a game, or a news item. Now, form an opinion about the topic and write that down in just a few sentences.

②

Stage Fright

Overcoming stage fright and communication anxiety.

LESSON OBJECTIVES

- Understand the causes of stage fright.
- Understand how stage fright affects your ability to communicate.
- Learn to control stage fright.
- Prepare, practice, and deliver your speeches.

PRINCIPLES

2.1. Causes of stage fright

Stage fright is a special form of **social anxiety**. When you are the focus of attention of a group of people, you are afraid of the *possibility* of making a mistake that will embarrass you. You hope to impress the audience with your speech, but at the same time want to avoid the possibility of embarrassment. Since the fear of embarrassment is very strong, you refuse to get on the stage and address the audience. That is the effect of stage fright.

You feel stage fright also as a "**choking effect**." You feel your voice is choked in your throat and you forget your speech. At that point,

Photo by Mohamed Hassan from Pixabay

you just want to run away from the stage and hide from the audience. You may feel your hands shaking and palms sweating.

You can overcome all these effects of stage fright by learning to **express confidence** through your appearance, voice, and expressions. Practicing the speech very well, especially the beginning part, is a necessary first step to control stage fright. Every single time you do a speech in front of an audience, small or large, your confidence and stage comfort will improve.

PRINCIPLES

2.2. Ways to control stage fright

Stage fright is also called "butterflies in the stomach." Think about some of your own reasons for stage fright. Do you feel more stage fright in front of a large audience or small one? Do you feel more stage fright if the audience are strangers or if they are friends? Do you feel more stage fright when you are well prepared or ill prepared?

There are two very effective ways to overcome stage fright:

1.   Perform speeches regularly at every opportunity that you get. This will create a new confidence pattern in your mind.

2.   Prepare and practice your speech really well before the performance. This will put your mind at ease.

Squirrels in the city are usually not afraid of people unlike the squirrels in the country. This is because the city squirrels are always exposed to people. In other words, the city squirrels overcame their stage fright through their continuous performance in front of people. Similarly, you can overcome your stage fright by making use of all opportunities you get for stage and classroom performances.

you can reduce your stage fright by preparing and practicing your speech way ahead of time. So, don't wait around until the last minute to prepare and practice.

Stage fright increases as you approach the time for your speech and it is at the peak in the first minute of your speech. So, preparing extremely well for the first minute helps you to control your stage fright.

Social embarrassment damages our social stature. This is why we fear such embarrassment and try avoiding situations that can cause them. Preparing and practicing the speech not only minimizes the possibility of any embarrassment while delivering it, but also increases our social stature.

"When I hear the audience clapping their hands at the end of my speech, a happy feeling comes all over me. I like that feeling. So, I want to do more public speaking."

Nikki, 6th Grade, Former Public Speaking Student
Bethesda, Maryland

SPEECH ASSIGNMENT

Grades 1-4

Speech Topic: **My first time playing soccer (or riding a bicycle or swimming.)**
Speech Objective: **In this speech, you will be sharing with the audience your first time experience with a sport. Share the memories and tell the stories of your first time experience.**
Speech Length: **1 minute**

Research and Critical Thinking

- Decide which sport you want to talk about.
- Try to remember your first time experience.
- How did you feel before you started playing? Afraid? Confused? Happy? Excited?
- Were there any funny moments on your first day?
- How long did it take you to become comfortable with the sport?
- How comfortable are you with it now? Do you enjoy it now?

Speech Structure

INTRODUCTION

- Address the audience.
- Give a short introduction on the topic.
- You can start with the story of a funny memory from the play ground. OR
- You can start with a question to the audience.

BODY

- Address some or all of the questions in the *Research and Critical Thinking* section.

CONCLUSION

- Give a short conclusion summarizing your main point. Your main point is that it takes regular practice to become a good player/to get bicycle balance/to become a comfortable swimmer.
- Thank the audience.

Stage Fright

Photo by Aaron Blanco Tejedor

SPEECH ASSIGNMENT

Grades 5-12

Speech Topic: **My favorite cultural festival**

Speech Objective: **Inform the audience about a cultural festival that you practice, its history, and it's social value.**

Speech Length: **1-2 minutes**

Research and Critical Thinking

- Examples of cultural festivals: Thanksgiving, Diwali, or Chinese new year.
- Which festival do you want to talk about?
- What is the history of this festival?
- What are the traditions related to this festival?
- Do you or your family have some special activities that you do during this festival?
- What are some of the recent personal experiences related to this festival?
- Why is this your favorite festival?

Speech Structure

INTRODUCTION

- Address the audience.
- Introduce the topic in an interesting way.

BODY

- Address some or all of the questions in the *Research and Critical Thinking* section.

CONCLUSION

- State the main idea that you want the audience to remember.
- Thank the audience.

A NEW WORD TO USE IN YOUR SPEECH

heritage

Meaning: Valued objects and qualities that are part of tradition or passed down from previous generations.

Example: Cultural festivals create a bond among people who share the same heritage.

PUBLIC SPEAKING BEGINNER

HOW TO PRESENT THE SPEECH

Enter the stage with a smile.

Display confidence in your steps.

Keep eye contact with the audience.

Control unnecessary body movements. Your speech is not only the ideas and spoken words, but also the way you express them to the audience. Your body language also speaks to the audience.

Speak up. Without having a good voice level, you won't be able to do voice modulation.

SPEECH OUTLINE

Speech Title:

Through Line: Write the main idea of your speech in one or two sentences.

Introduction: Present your topic in an interesting way to hook the audience.

Body - Point 1: The idea, data, and examples.

Body - Point 2: The idea, data, and examples.

Conclusion: The main point that you want your audience to remember.

QUESTIONS AND EXERCISES

1   What are the causes of stage fright?

2   What steps can you take to control your stage fright?

3   Why are squirrels in the city show no fear of people while squirrels in the country run away from people?

We feel the maximum level of stage fright at the beginning of the speech.

Photo by Sammie Vasquiez

Presentation literacy is a core skill for the twenty-first century. It's the most impactful way to share who you are and what you care about. If you can learn to do it, your self-confidence will flourish, and you may be amazed at the beneficial impact it can have on your success in life.

Chris Anderson

Confidence

"Fake it till you make it."

LESSON OBJECTIVES

- How to show confidence on stage.
- How to develop confidence for class participation and group discussions.
- Understand how the outward display of confidence can improve the internal feeling of confidence.
- Prepare, practice, and deliver your speeches.

Photo by Hust Wilson

Take advantage of every opportunity to practice your communication skills so that when important occasions arise, you will have the gift, the style, the sharpness, the clarity, and the emotions to affect other people.

Jim Rohn

PRINCIPLES

3.1. The psychology of confidence building

Your brain is capable of building resilience by taking cues from your actions. In other words, the actions you take send signals to your brain that will create emotions corresponding to those actions. Most people are familiar with the concept of actions following emotions, but not the other way around. For example, you feel anger first and then act angrily. But new research shows that you can act angrily which in turn makes you feel angry. So, purposely taking actions first can generate the corresponding emotions that you would like to have.

You can use this psychological process for confidence building. You may have heard the phrase, "**fake it till you make it**" and "**fake it till you become it.**" Both phrases point to the fact that by faking confidence in public speaking and communication you can truly become more self-confident.

3.2. How to show confidence

Fake it till you make it... and fake it till you become it... should be your motto for developing public speaking confidence.

Think about ways to display confidence. It involves how you walk, stand, look, and speak. It involves your facial expressions and hand gestures. It involves your voice and tone.

How do you fake confidence? There are several things you can do to appear as a confident speaker even when you feel stage fright.

Take firm, confident steps when you enter the stage.

Look at the audience.

Smile, if the speech occasion is appropriate for it.

Control unnecessary body movements.

Speak up.

And most importantly, **practice your speech until you are comfortable with it's flow**.

Taking these steps for every speech you do will build-up your self-confidence. It will also help you form a better public speaking style.

Skill for class participation and participation in group discussions is formed through habits. Every time students shy away from such opportunities, they are forming a new habit of non-participation. When teachers ask questions in the class, raise your hand to, at least, give a one word answer. Gradually, this practice will form a new habit in you: a habit of confidence in class participation.

SPEECH ASSIGNMENT

Grades 1-4

Speech Topic: **Story of my hometown**

Speech Objective: **Inform the audience the history and the present state of your hometown.**

Speech Length: **1 minute**

Research and Critical Thinking

- What hometown would you like to speak about? It doesn't have to be where you live now.
- What is the story behind the name of your hometown?
- When was it founded?
- What do you know about its history?
- What do you like and dislike about your hometown?
- What are some of the interesting facts about your hometown?

Speech Structure

INTRODUCTION

- Start with an interesting fact about your hometown.

BODY

- Address some or all of the questions listed in the *Research and Critical Thinking* section.

CONCLUSION

- End with another interesting fact about your hometown.
- Thank the audience.

Photo by Tomas Halajcik

SPEECH ASSIGNMENT

Grades 5-12

Speech Topic: **Stars, Planets, and Us.**

Speech Objective: **Prepare and present a speech about a few things you have learned in school or read in books on stars, planets, earth, and the living things like plants and animals.**

Speech Length: **1-2 minutes**

Research and Critical Thinking

- What are stars?
- What are planets?
- What are the planets in the solar system?
- Why can't we live on any planes other than earth?
- What are some interesting facts about a few planets?
- Do you know of any new research and discoveries in this field?
- What have you learned about animals and plants?

Speech Structure

INTRODUCTION

- Address the audience.
- Give a short introduction on the topic and create a hook by talking about some interesting facts about stars, planets, or human beings OR asking a question to the audience.

BODY

- Answer some or all of the questions in the *Research and Critical Thinking* section.

CONCLUSION

- Give a short conclusion summarizing your main points.
- Thank the audience.

A NEW WORD TO USE IN YOUR SPEECH

pandemonium

Meaning: A wild uproar.

Example: Pandemonium erupted in the auditorium as the young student delivered a speech with confidence.

HOW TO PRESENT THE SPEECH

Enter the stage with a smile.

Display confidence in your steps.

Keep eye contact with the audience.

Control unnecessary body movements.

Speak up and use voice modulation.

Keep a good body posture. Posture displays confidence.

SPEECH OUTLINE

Speech Title:

Through Line: Write the main idea of your speech in one or two sentences.

Introduction: Present your topic in an interesting way to hook the audience.

Body - Point 1: The idea, data, and examples.

Body - Point 2: The idea, data, and examples.

Conclusion: The main point that you want your audience to remember.

QUESTIONS AND EXERCISES

1 What are some of the ways to show confidence?

2 Why do you think "faking confidence" is a good technique for "making confidence"?

3 What expressions of a speaker indicate to you the speaker has lack of confidence? (This will help you create your own plans for showing confidence to the audience.)

"One thing I like about public speaking is the increasing self-confidence I get after each performance. After each speech, I feel more comfortable to do it again."

Sophia, 7th Grade, Former Public Speaking Student Centreville, Virginia

On stage, you are alone. It's your performance and yours only.

Photo by Ian Froome

Posture

Good body posture and power pose show confidence to your audience.

LESSON OBJECTIVES

- Understand how posture is part of your "speech expression."
- Practice power pose for communication.
- Practice good standing posture for delivering speeches.
- Prepare, practice, and deliver your speeches.

Photo by Wade Austin Ellis

PRINCIPLES

4.1. Power Pose

Posture is the way you hold your body when standing or sitting. In public speaking, as you stand on the stage, posture is an important aspect of how you present yourself to the audiences. Psychological studies demonstrated that posture plays an important role in nonverbal communication and good posture is important for creating a good connection with the audiences. Body posture and movements not only send nonverbal communication to others, but also they affect the emotions of the speaker. A good posture can improve your self-confidence.

Power pose, a good straight posture with shoulders up, presents you as a speaker who has confidence. On the other hand, a sluggish posture with droopy shoulders sends the signal of low energy to the audience.

Proper feet positioning is another factor to pay attention to because it affects your posture.

- **Stand in the middle of the stage if possible.**
- **Keep your feet pointing straight to the audience. If you put your foot out in any angle, your body will turn to that side.**
- **Stand with your shoulders up.**
- **Control unnecessary body movements.**
- **Don't play with your clothing or notes in your hand because it can distract your audience.**

4.2. Standing Posture

Good standing posture is an important part of your "speech expression." You should practice good posture and confident body gestures all the time not just for public speaking. Your standing posture will also help you build the connection with the audience by showing them your enthusiasm for the speech and consideration to the audience.

Good posture is also good for your health and it allows you to have more energy for your speech and all types of communication.

The most important thing in communication is to hear what isn't being said.

Peter Drucker

SPEECH ASSIGNMENT

Grades 1-4

Speech Topic: **How to plan a party**

Speech Objective: **The objective of this speech is to give instructions to your classmates on planning a party.**

Speech Length: **1 minute**

Research and Critical Thinking

- What are the things you need to consider when planning a party?
- Is there a theme for your party? (Birthday, Halloween, Summer, etc.)
- Whom are you inviting?
- What food are you planning to serve?
- Where will you hold the party?
- What entertainments will be provided?
- What other arrangements are needed?
- Who will do the cleanup after the party?

Speech Structure

INTRODUCTION

- Address the audience
- Tell the audience about a party that you have recently attended.
- Tell them about what you liked and disliked about that party.

BODY

- Do you have any experience with planning parties?
- What are your advice for the audience?
- Address some or all of the questions in the *Research and Critical Thinking* section.

CONCLUSION

- Thank the audience

Photo by Adi Goldstein

SPEECH ASSIGNMENT

Grades 5-12

Speech Topic: **Earthquake**

Speech Objective: **Inform the audience how earthquakes happen and what we can do to protect ourselves from the damages.**

Speech Length: **1-2 minutes**

Research and Critical Thinking

- How does earthquake happen?
- How do we measure it?
- Are there any earthquakes that happened recently?
- Are there any human experience stories about earthquake that you can tell?
- Are there any precautions that we can take to protect us?
- What new some new research on this topic?
- What is the main focus of your speech? (The science of earthquake or the sufferings from earthquake or the research in the field of earthquake.)

Speech Structure

INTRODUCTION

- Start with an interesting fact or story.

BODY

- Address some or all of the questions in the *Research and Critical Thinking* section.

CONCLUSION

- End with an interesting fact about your main focus of the speech.
- Thank the audience.

A NEW WORD TO USE IN YOUR SPEECH

subterranean

Meaning: Underground.

Example: Earthquake can destroy skyscrapers and subterranean structures like subway.

HOW TO PRESENT THE SPEECH

Enter the stage with confident steps.

Smile.

Keep eye contact with the audience.

Control unnecessary body movements.

Speak up and use voice modulation.

Present yourself in power pose.

SPEECH OUTLINE

Speech Title:

Through Line: Write the main idea of your speech in one or two sentences.

Introduction: Present your topic in an interesting way to hook the audience.

Body - Point 1: The idea, data, and examples.

Body - Point 2: The idea, data, and examples.

Conclusion: The main point that you want your audience to remember.

QUESTIONS AND EXERCISES

1   What is good posture and bad posture?

2   What are the unnecessary body movements that some new public speaking students make?

3   What is Power Pose? What are the benefits of power pose in public speaking?

4   Practice good standing posture. Pay attention to how your shoulders and neck feel in that pose.

The speaker shows confidence through her smile, posture, and hand gestures.

Photo by Raw Pixels

PUBLIC SPEAKING BEGINNER

Confident Steps

Importance of showing confidence in the manner of walking.

LESSON OBJECTIVES

- Learn to display confidence and power through the way of walking.
- Understand how body movements send nonverbal signals to audience.
- Prepare, practice, and deliver your speeches.

On speaking, first have something to say, second say it, third stop when you have said it, and finally give it an accurate title.

John Shaw Billings

Photo by Lindsay Henwood

PRINCIPLES

5.1. Walking with confidence

Audience are watching you as you walk to the podium to present your speech. The way you walk, which is also called gait, is one of the first things your audience will notice. Your enthusiasm and energy are visible to the audience from your gait and so present yourself in the best possible way to express high enthusiasm and high energy. Take firm, confident steps when you come to the podium.

The way you stand on the stage also sends non-verbal signals to your audience. All those signals should carry the message of confidence. Another factor you should pay attention to is the way you dress because your appearance does influence the audience.

If you pace on the stage as you deliver your speech, keep facing the audience and avoid turning your back to them.

You should be careful about showing too much excitement in your steps. There were times when the speaker fell down on the stage because of careless movements. An untied shoelace or a slippery floor can ruin your planned grand entry to the stage. Remember, when you present your speech, you are performing and so plan your movements as in a performance.

"A couple of things I like about public speaking are: one, I can be a more outgoing person and two, people would look at me with admiration.."

Julia, 5th Grade
Ashburn, Virginia

SPEECH ASSIGNMENT

Grades 1-4

Speech Topic: **If you could become an animal for a day, which animal you would like to be?**

Speech Objective: **In this speech, you will be sharing with the audience information about an animal and how you like to get some of its capabilities.**

Speech Length: **1 minute**

Research and Critical Thinking

- Select an animal to speak about.
  - Where does it live?
  - What are its characteristics?
  - What are the qualities in this animal that attracted you?
  - Have you ever seen this animal?
  - What is its social life like?

Speech Structure

INTRODUCTION

- Address the audience.
- Create a hook by telling the audience a joke, riddle, or story about this animal.

BODY

- Answer some or all of the questions in the *Research and Critical Thinking* section.

CONCLUSION

- Emphasize the main point of your speech one more time.
- Thank the audience.

Photo by Nikolay Tchaouchev

SPEECH ASSIGNMENT

Grades 5-12

Speech Topic: **School Uniforms**

Speech Objective: **Present your point of view on school uniforms and convince the audience why your arguments are correct.**

Speech Length: **1-2 minutes**

Research and Critical Thinking

- Define what school uniforms are?
- What is the purpose of it?
- Is it a good idea or not?
- If there are good intentions for making all students wear uniforms, are those intentions achieved?
- What are the problems with school uniforms?
- Do you or any of your friends have personal experiences with school uniforms? What are those experiences?
- What is your thesis statement or the main idea of this speech?

Speech Structure

INTRODUCTION

- Start with an interesting fact or story.

BODY

- Address some or all of the questions in the *Research and Critical Thinking* section.

CONCLUSION

- End with your main point of the speech, but stated in a different way.
- Thank the audience.

A NEW WORD TO USE IN YOUR SPEECH

persevere

Meaning: To keep at something in spite of difficulties.

Example: Students persevered and developed good public speaking style.

HOW TO PRESENT THE SPEECH

Walk to the stage with **confident steps.**

Keep a **power pose** and control unnecessary body movements.

Use **hand gestures** to express your ideas. Keep your hands in the **power circle.**

Keep **eye contact** with the audience.

Speak up and use **voice modulation.**

SPEECH OUTLINE

Speech Title:

Through Line: Write the main idea of your speech in one or two sentences.

Introduction: Present your topic in an interesting way to hook the audience.

Body - Point 1: The idea, data, and examples.

Body - Point 2: The idea, data, and examples.

Conclusion: The main point that you want your audience to remember.

QUESTIONS AND EXERCISES

1   What does confidence in steps mean?

2   What factors other than the speech itself are important in influencing the audience?

Facial expression that radiates confidence

Photo by Raw Pixel

6

Gestures

Gestures, especially hand gestures, are important to nonverbal communication.

LESSON OBJECTIVES

- Learn the importance of hand gestures in communication.
- Practice good hand gestures to express your ideas with power.
- Prepare, practice, and deliver your speeches.

To speak well supposes a habit of attention which shows itself in the thought; by language we learn to think and above all to develop thought.

Carl Victor De Bonstetten

PRINCIPLES

6.1. Importance of gestures

Hand and body gestures improve the effect of communication. So, use your hand and body gestures to create a powerful impact on your audience.

Use hand gestures as you usually use them in conversations. That way, the audience will feel that your movements are natural. Unless used carefully, your hand and body gestures can also distract the audience.

6.2. Evolution and gestures

Ancestors of Homo Sapiens communicated through gestures, sounds, and expressions for millions of years. Then about 100,000 years ago, Homo Sapiens developed the capability for a structured language-based communication, which made them the most powerful species ever lived on earth. Their power comes from the capability they gained by the use of language and communication to coordinate the efforts of thousands of people to engage them in collaborative work even when none of them knew each other.

Why do we feel emotionally connected with hurricane victims in another state or root for soccer players from another country even though we don't

know any of them? It is because we are connected with them through language. Language created a network where we and the hurricane victims and the soccer players share the same emotional thread.

Millions or years of evolution hardwired the capability for gesture-based communication in our genes. This is why facial expressions for happiness, anger, or boredom are universal. Irrespective of the country or culture of people, we are able to tell very quickly what their facial expressions and body language mean.

Using facial expressions, body language, and gestures in public speaking will send powerful signals of meaning and emotion to your audience.

- Bring up your hands to the power circle, which is large circle with its top at your forehead and bottom at your naval. Your hand gestures in this circle will appear as powerful and expansive gestures.
- Keep a firm wrist and make sure that your gestures are coming from your hands, and not from your palms.
- Avoid finger pointing to the audience. When necessary to point, use hand pointing instead.
- Avoid playing with fingers and clothing, which is common among new public speaking students.
- Do not hide your hands in your pocket or behind your back.

SPEECH ASSIGNMENT

Grades 1-4

Speech Topic: **Teach to play a game.**
Speech Objective: **The objective of this exercise is to teach or coach the students to play a game.**
Speech Length: **1 minute**

Research and Critical Thinking

- Identify a board game, video game, sports, or any other type of game which you can play with others.
- What are the rules of this game?
- What is the objective of the game?
- How many people are needed to play it?
- How do you play it? Explain in a step-by-step manner.
- Ask for volunteers from the class to demonstrate how to play the game.

Speech Structure

INTRODUCTION
- Address the audience.
- Give a brief explanation along with the objectives of the game.

BODY
- Explain the steps of playing the game.
- Demonstrate how to play the game either alone or with volunteers.

CONCLUSION
- Ask if anyone has any questions.
- Thank the audience.

Smile and Victory Symbol

Photo by Larm Rmah

SPEECH ASSIGNMENT

Grades 5-12

Speech Topic: **"Be the change that you would like to see in the world."**

Speech Objective: **Present your point of view on this quote by Mahatma Gandhi.**

Speech Length: **1-2 minutes**

Research and Critical Thinking

- What is the story behind this quote?
- What does this quote mean?
- How can we practice it?
- Are there any examples or personal stories related to this quote that you can tell?
- Are there any related quotes that support this idea?
- Are there leaders other than Gandhi who practiced this in their life?

Speech Structure

INTRODUCTION

- Start with an interesting fact or story.

BODY

- Address some or all of the questions in the *Research and Critical Thinking* section.

CONCLUSION

- End with your inspirational message.
- Thank the audience.

A NEW WORD TO USE IN YOUR SPEECH

sustenance

Meaning: Something that gives you support or strength, physically or mentally.

Example: It is easier to make changes to your life when close friends offer sustenance.

HOW TO PRESENT THE SPEECH

Walk to the stage with **confident steps.**

Keep a **power pose** and control unnecessary body movements.

Use **hand gestures** to express your ideas. Keep your hands in the **power circle**.

Keep **eye contact** with the audience.

Speak up and use **voice modulation.**

Speak with **pauses**.

KEYNOTE SPEECH ASSIGNMENT

During the next few weeks, you will work progressively on developing a 3-4 minute speech (2-3 pages), which will be your keynote speech for the completion of the Beginner Level Public Speaking Training Program. This is a speech on a topic of your selection. Each week, you develop the speech gradually by following the instructions given in the workbook under the Keynote Speech section.

- Select a general topic area for your keynote speech; a topic that you are passionate about will be easier to develop. You will present this speech at the end of the Beginner Level classes.
- Discuss the topic with the instructor.

KEYNOTE SPEECH PLANNING

Topic Area:
Possible Topic 1:
Possible Topic 2:

QUESTIONS AND EXERCISES

1   How evolution programmed gesture-based communication in us?

2   What are the main things to remember when practicing hand gestures?

SPEECH OUTLINE

Speech Title:

_____

Through Line: Write the main idea of your speech in one or two sentences.

_____

_____

Introduction: Present your topic in an interesting way to hook the audience.

_____

Body - Point 1: The idea, data, and examples.

_____

_____

Body - Point 2: The idea, data, and examples.

_____

_____

Conclusion: The main point that you want your audience to remember.

_____

_____

PUBLIC SPEAKING BEGINNER

Facial Expressions

Facial expressions convey the emotions of communication.

> In order to speak short upon any subject, think long.
>
> **H. H. Brackenridge**

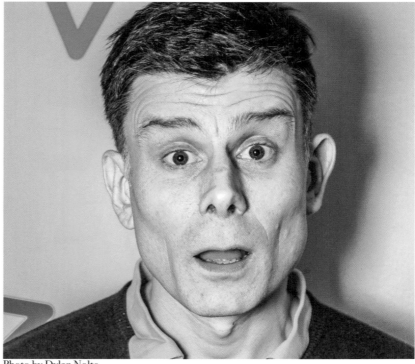

Photo by Dylan Nolte

PRINCIPLES

7.1. Importance of facial expressions

Emotions are conveyed from the speaker to the audience through multiple ways. Words, tone, body language, and facial expressions convey the emotions of communication in different degrees. Of these, facial expressions carry the highest level of emotional content when audience can see the face of the speaker such as in an in-person speech or a televised one. Since audience are looking at the face of the speaker, the expressions on the face become an effective means of communication for the speaker to use.

"**Mirror neurons**" in our brain and its functions are a recent discovery. Mirror neurons help us feel what others feel. These neurons "mirror" the emotions of others by getting their cues from sources such as facial expressions. Hence, in a speech, it is important for the speaker to spark a response of the mirror neurons of the audience. The most effective means to do that is by the use of facial expressions.

In communication, whether it is public speaking or interpersonal, words carry the message and facial and body expressions and tone convey the emotions.

- **During speech practice, it is important to try different facial expressions that correspond to the tone of your voice.**
- **If appropriate for the topic, having a smile on your face as you come to the stage will not only help you connect better with the audience, but also boost your self-confidence.**
- **Within the same speech, you may need your audience to feel different emotions and hence try different facial expressions.**
- **After a humorous comment, a pause and a smile could lead the audience to laughter.**

Photo by Raw Pixel

SPEECH ASSIGNMENT

Grades 1-4

Speech Topic: **My favorite childhood toy and song.**

Speech Objective: **Tell the audience about some of your favorite things from the past, specifically about a childhood toy and a song.**

Speech Length: **1 minute**

Research and Critical Thinking

- What was the favorite toy that you had when you were young.
- What was your favorite song from your young age?
- Explain your way of playing with the toy.
- Explain what happened to the toy. Do you still have it?
- Did you ever lose the toy and later found it? Explain the emotions you felt when you lost the toy and when you found it.
- Sing that favorite song of yours from the past, if you can. Otherwise, just tell the audience what the song was.
- Do you remember any special thing about the toy or the song?

Speech Structure

INTRODUCTION

- Address the audience.
- Give a short introduction that will get the audience's attention. You can start with a story about the toy - how did you get it or how did you get attached to it.

Photo by Vanessa Bucceri

BODY

- Address some or all of the questions from the *Research and Critical Thinking* section.

CONCLUSION

- Emphasize the main point of your speech one more time.
- Thank the audience.

SPEECH ASSIGNMENT

Grades 5-12

Speech Topic: **Global Warming**

Speech Objective: **Inform the audience about the dangers of global warming and encourage them for actions. This is a "call to action" speech.**

Speech Length: **1-2 minutes**

Research and Critical Thinking

- What is global warming?
- What are the causes of global warming?
- How will it affect the world?
- What can we do about it?

Speech Structure

INTRODUCTION

- Present a catchy title.
- Address the audience.

BODY

- Organize the speech using the following prompts:
  - What? (What is the issue on hand?)
  - So What? (What are the implications of the issue?)
  - Now What? (What should we do about it?)
- Create sound bites or phrases that can be repeated throughout your speech.

CONCLUSION

- End with emphasizing your call to action.
- Thank the audience.

A NEW WORD TO USE IN YOUR SPEECH

catastrophe

Meaning: A very big tragic event or ruin.

Example: The effect of global warming is going to be catastrophic for every living thing on earth, unless controlled effectively.

HOW TO PRESENT THE SPEECH

Walk to the stage with **confident steps.**

Keep a **power pose** and control unnecessary body movements.

Use **hand gestures** to express your ideas. Keep your hands in the **power circle.**

Keep **eye contact** with the audience.

Speak up, with pauses, and variation in your tone and pace.

Speak with **pauses.**

KEYNOTE SPEECH ASSIGNMENT

- Select a topic for your keynote speech.
- Discuss the topic with the instructor.
- Based on the instructor's feedback, decide on a specific speech topic.
- Prepare a thesis statement. In one or two sentences explain the main idea (the central theme) of your speech.

KEYNOTE SPEECH PLANNING

Speech Topic:

Thesis Statement (Thorough line):

DISCUSSION QUESTIONS

1   What are some of the emotions that produce similar facial expressions among people from different countries and cultures?

2   Can you identify some gestures or expressions that mean opposite things in different countries or cultures?

SPEECH OUTLINE

Speech Title:

Through Line: Write the main idea of your speech in one or two sentences.

Introduction: Present your topic in an interesting way to hook the audience.

Body - Point 1: The idea, data, and examples.

Body - Point 2: The idea, data, and examples.

Conclusion: The main point that you want your audience to remember.

Eye Contact

Eye contact connects the speaker with the audience.

LESSON OBJECTIVES

- Understand the importance of eye contact in communication.
- Practice eye contact with the audience.
- Prepare, practice, and deliver your speeches.

Photo by Linus Schutz

PRINCIPLES

8.1. Importance of eye contact

Without keeping eye contact, it is very difficult to make connection with the audience; and connection with the audience is an important factor to present a successful speech. To make your audience feel that you are talking to them, keep eye contact with them throughout the speech. In other words, speak to the audience, not over them.

Eye contact with the audience gives you a continuous feedback on how well they are enjoying your speech. You can see the enjoyment, the excitement, and all sorts of responses on their face. Public speaking is a dynamic process; it will be most effective when you can adjust and change your performance based on the feedback that you observe on your audiences.

In public speaking and interpersonal communication, eye contact is one of the most important factor necessary to build a good connection between the speaker and the listener(s).

> There are three things to aim at in public speaking: first to get into your subject, then to get your subject into yourself, and lastly, to get your subject into your hearers.
>
> **A. S. Gregg**

- In all your communication, on-stage and off-stage, practice direct eye contact with the audience so that it will become part of your speaking habits.
- For small meetings where you stand closer to your audience, look directly at each member of the audience for about 3-7 seconds before moving your eye contact to the next person.
- For events in large auditoriums where you stand on a raised stage, look at different sections of the audience rather than individuals.
- Pay attention to not develop the habit of looking only at one person or one section in the audience.
- For televised speeches, you should be looking at the camera so that audience can see it as a direct eye contact with them.

SPEECH ASSIGNMENT

Grades 1-4

Speech Topic: **Life of a butterfly**

Speech Objective: **Teach the audience about the life of a butterfly and some interesting facts.**

Speech Length: **1 minute**

Research and Critical Thinking:

- What are the different stages in the life of a butterfly?
- What are the different types of butterflies that we usually see?
- What are some interesting facts about butterflies?
- Are there visual aids (pictures) that you can use?

Speech Structure

INTRODUCTION

- Address the audience.
- To create a hook, either speak about an interesting fact about butterflies or speak about a personal experience that you had with them.

BODY

- Explain what you have learned from your research on butterflies.

CONCLUSION

- Speak about another interesting fact about butterflies.
- Thank the audience.

Photo by Krzysztof Niewolny

SPEECH ASSIGNMENT

Grades 5-12

Speech Topic: **Collaborative Life of Bees**

Speech Objective: **Teach the audience about the collaborative life of bees.**

Speech Length: **1-2 minutes**

Research and Critical Thinking

- What are the different types of bees?
- Explain bees colony and bee hives.
- Explain the roles of Queen bee and the other types of bees in a colony.
- How is honey produced?
- Explain the dangers of bee stings and allergy.

Speech Structure

INTRODUCTION

- Present a catchy title.
- Address the audience.
- Create a hook by talking about a personal experience that had with bees.

BODY

- Organize and present your research in the simplest manner so that you can explain the information easily.
- Add stories and interesting facts to make the points memorable.

CONCLUSION

- Ask students one or two questions.
- Ask them if they have any questions for you.
- Thank the audience.

A NEW WORD TO USE IN YOUR SPEECH

servile

Meaning: suitable to a servant.

Example: Worker bees behavior is servile with no practical independence.

HOW TO PRESENT THE SPEECH

Walk to the stage with **confident steps.**

Keep a **power pose** and control unnecessary body movements.

Use **hand gestures** to express your ideas. Keep your hands in the **power circle**.

Keep **eye contact** with the audience.

Speak up, with pauses, and variation in your tone and pace.

Speak with **pauses.**

Control **mannerisms**, the "ahs" and "ums"

KEYNOTE SPEECH ASSIGNMENT

- Select a topic for your keynote speech.
- Discuss the topic with the instructor.
- Based on the instructor's feedback, decide on a specific speech topic.
- Prepare a thesis statement. In one or two sentences explain the main idea (the central theme) of your speech.
- Create a list of all the points that you can think of and everything that you can find from research. Just list the points only, not the details.
- Discuss with the instructor to identify the main points that should be included in your speech.

KEYNOTE SPEECH PLANNING

Speech Points	

QUESTIONS AND EXERCISES

1   Why is eye contact important in communication?

2   What are some of the reasons for speakers not keeping eye contact with the audience?

3   What is the best way to develop the habit of eye contact?

SPEECH OUTLINE

Speech Title:

Through Line: Write the main idea of your speech in one or two sentences.

Introduction: Present your topic in an interesting way to hook the audience.

Body - Point 1: The idea, data, and examples.

Body - Point 2: The idea, data, and examples.

Conclusion: The main point that you want your audience to remember.

Speak Up: Volume and Pitch

Proper volume and pitch are necessary to create voice impact.

LESSON OBJECTIVES

- Understand the characteristics of voice such as volume and pitch.
- Learn about voice modulation and how it impacts public speaking effectiveness.
- Practice speaking up.
- Prepare, practice, and deliver your speeches.

> Talking and eloquence are not the same: to speak, and to speak well are two things. A fool may talk, but a wise man speaks.
>
> **Ben Jonson**

Photo by Obafemi Moyosade

PRINCIPLES

9.1. Uniqueness of sound

Your voice is unique, and you should be proud of it. All of us sound different from each other. That is part of our personality and identity. If you record your voice using a voice recorder and play it back, you may be surprised to hear a voice slightly different from what you are used to. That's because when you speak, your sound vibrations travel to your ears not only through the air but also through your jaws. But your sound others are familiar with is what you hear from the recording device.

Voice modulation, the ups and downs in your voice increases the attractiveness of your speech. Voice modulation involves many other factors, such as tone, pitch, and pausing.

Photo by Clem Onojeghuo

- **Low voice is commonly considered as a sign of shyness and lack of confidence. So, to display confidence you should speak up.**
- **If you are speaking without a microphone, you should adjust the volume of your voice to the size of the audience so that all can hear you clearly.**
- **Using sound pitch that corresponds properly to the content of your speech can help you amplify the effect of the speech.**

SPEECH ASSIGNMENT

Grades 1-4

Speech Topic: **Why I want a pet.**
Speech Objective: **Convince the audience that you have good reasons to ask for a pet.**
Speech Length: **1 minute**

Research and Critical Thinking:

- What pet do you want?
- What benefits do you get by having a pet?
- What additional responsibilities do you plan to take on if you get a pet?
- Why do you think your parents would say NO to your request?
- What questions will your parents ask you?
- What are your answers for those questions and concerns?

Speech Structure

INTRODUCTION

- Address the audience.
- Create a hook by telling the audience how much you enjoyed when you played with someone else's pet in their house or when they brought their pet to your house. Now, transition to the body of the speech by telling the audience how that experience of playing with a pet made you feel that you also want to have one of your own.

BODY

- Address some or all of the questions in the *Research and Critical Thinking* section.

CONCLUSION

- Summarize your main points. Your main theme of the speech is the benefits of having a pet.
- Thank the audience.

Photo by iPet Photos

SPEECH ASSIGNMENT

Grades 5-12

Speech Topic: **Improving our school cafeteria.**

Speech Objective: **Present the results of a research that you did on your school cafeteria. Present the report in the form of a speech and convince the audience to accept your recommendations.**

Research and Critical Thinking

- What is the current state of your school cafeteria?
- Do you think it needs improvement?
- What stories and experiences do you have that will support your argument?
- What do you think about the food quality? Nutritional balance? Selections available? Cost and wastage? Cleanliness? Cafeteria Staff? Lunch timing?
- What recommendations do you have?
- What benefits do you see if the school implements your recommendations?
- Do you have any data and statistics to support your position?

Speech Structure

- Create a catchy title.
- INTRODUCTION
  - Hook the audience with a personal experience story.
- BODY
  - Present your research in the best order. You may use "problem and solution" style by describing each problem and its solution. Use statistics and data to support your position.
- CONCLUSION
  - Summarize your recommendations.
  - Thank the audience

A NEW WORD TO USE IN YOUR SPEECH

inhospitable

Meaning: unfriendly, unfavorable, not welcoming.

Example: Inhospitable atmosphere in the cafeteria makes me not wanting to go there at all.

HOW TO PRESENT THE SPEECH

Walk to the stage with **confident steps.**

Keep a **power pose** and control unnecessary body movements.

Use **hand gestures** to express your ideas. Keep your hands in the **power circle**.

Keep **eye contact** with the audience.

Speak up, with pauses, and variation in your tone and pace.

Speak with **pauses**.

Control **mannerisms**, the "ahs" and "ums"

KEYNOTE SPEECH ASSIGNMENT

- Select a topic for your keynote speech.
- Discuss the topic with the instructor.
- Based on the instructor's feedback, decide on a specific speech topic.
- Prepare a thesis statement. In one or two sentences explain the main idea (the central theme) of your speech.
- Create a brain dump or in other words, create a list of all the points that you can think of and everything that you can find from research. Just list the points only, not the details.
- Discuss with the instructor to identify the main points that should be included in your speech. These are the points that would support your thesis.
- Find some stories and examples to support the points you have identified.
- Write the first paragraph of the body of the speech.

"I used to not look at the audience because I was always afraid that they would laugh at me and I would forget what to say. After the training at YSC, now I am very comfortable to keep eye contact with the audience."

James, 7th grade, Former YSC Student
Chantilly, Virginia

QUESTIONS AND EXERCISES

1 What is voice modulation?

2 Why is speaking up an important factor in effective communication?

SPEECH OUTLINE

Speech Title:

Through Line: Write the main idea of your speech in one or two sentences.

Introduction: Present your topic in an interesting way to hook the audience.

Body - Point 1: The idea, data, and examples.

Body - Point 2: The idea, data, and examples.

Conclusion: The main point that you want your audience to remember.

Tone and Diction

Proper tone and diction carry the emotions of the speech.

> The two words, information and communication, are often used interchangeably, but they signify quite different things. Information is giving out; communication is getting through.
>
> **Sydney Harris**

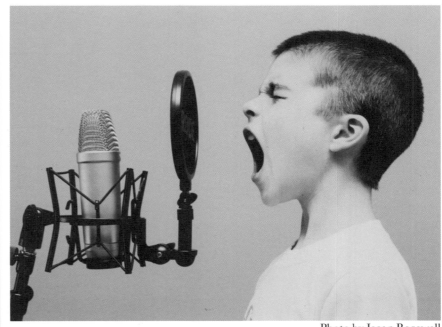

Photo by Jason Rosewell

PRINCIPLES

10.1. Tone and Diction

Tone is the emotion in your voice – the feeling that you are trying to convey. If you are passionate about the topic of your speech, your emotions will come through as tone variations in your speech. Once you know what emotions you want to generate in your audience, plan the tone appropriately within your speech.

Diction refers to the use of appropriate words and phrases to convey meaning. There are several words that sound alike, but of different meaning. So, the style of pronouncing such words must be carefully considered.

- **Tone and pitch of your voice carry emotions. So, it is important to practice the speech with appropriate tone and pitch so that you can bring out vocally the emotions associated with your speech content.**
- **Remember, it is very difficult to modulate your voice if you speak in low voice. So, speak up.**

Photo by Seb Barsoumian

SPEECH ASSIGNMENT

Grades 1-4

Speech Topic: **A Story written by me.**

Speech Objective: **In this exercise, you will be telling a story that you have written. If you do not have a story that you've created, you can use a story that you've read or heard.**

Speech Length: **1 minute**

Research and Critical Thinking

- Start with creating the settings, characters, and their problem for your story.
- Build up the story through solving some of the problems, bringing in new characters, and bringing up new problems.
- Finally solve all the problems for the main character.

Speech Structure

- Address the audience.
- Announce the name of your story.
- Give a one or two sentence introduction of the story. (Example: "This is the story of an alien who came to earth - to a place in the United States - on a Thanksgiving day.)
- Stories should have a beginning-middle-end structure.
- Try voice modulation by changing the tone and pitch for different characters as you talk about them or present their conversations.
- Thank the audience.

Photo by Jonny Lindner (Pixabay)

SPEECH ASSIGNMENT

Grades 5-12

Speech Topic: **"A person must have a certain amount of intelligent ignorance to get anywhere." This is a quote by Charles Kettering.**
Speech Objective: **Prepare an inspirational speech on this quote and present your point of view.**
Speech Length: **1-2 minutes**

Research and Critical Thinking

- What does this quote mean?
- How can we practice it?
- Are there any examples or personal stories that you can tell on this quote?
- Are there any related quotes that support this idea?
- Are there any stories that you heard of any leaders who practiced this in their life?

Speech Structure

- INTRODUCTION
  - Start with an interesting fact or story.
- BODY
  - Address some or all of the questions in the *Research and Critical Thinking* section listed above.
- CONCLUSION
  - End with your inspirational message.
  - Thank the audience.

A NEW WORD TO USE IN YOUR SPEECH

enunciation

Meaning: The way of pronouncing or expressing something.

Example: The speaker's enunciation was very clear despite the fact that he was a foreigner.

HOW TO PRESENT THE SPEECH

Walk to the stage with **confident steps.**

Keep a **power pose** and control unnecessary body movements.

Use **hand gestures** to express your ideas. Keep your hands in the **power circle**.

Keep **eye contact** with the audience.

Speak up, with pauses, and variation in your tone and pace.

Speak with **pauses**.

Control **mannerisms**, the "ahs" and "ums"

KEYNOTE SPEECH ASSIGNMENT

- Select a topic.
- Prepare a thesis statement.
- Create a brain dump.
- Identify the main points.
- Find some stories and examples.
- Write the first paragraph.
- Write the rest of the speech.
- Develop the introduction and conclusion.

QUESTIONS AND EXERCISES

1   What is tone?

2   What is diction?

3   What are the three parts of a story?

SPEECH OUTLINE

Speech Title:

Through Line: Write the main idea of your speech in one or two sentences.

_____

_____

Introduction: Present your topic in an interesting way to hook the audience.

_____

Body - Point 1: The idea, data, and examples.

_____

_____

Body - Point 2: The idea, data, and examples.

_____

_____

Conclusion: The main point that you want your audience to remember.

_____

_____

Pace and Pause

Varying pace and proper pausing increase the emotional power of the speech.

LESSON OBJECTIVES

- Understand the importance of varying pace in the speech.
- Understand and practice how pausing adds power to the speech.
- Prepare, practice, and deliver your speeches.

Photo by WhoisLimos

PRINCIPLES

11.1. Speech Pace

Audio books usually use 150-160 words per minute pace. Although this rate is ideal for most listeners, speakers should employ the technique of varying the pace based on the content of the speech. Increasing the pace increases the suspense or tension while decreasing the pace puts listeners in a relaxed mood.

Within the first few minutes of the speech, audience will adjust to the speaker's normal pace and expect to see that pace to continue to the end. So, the variations of pace that the speaker introduce are elements that make the speech more exciting.

11.2. Pausing

Whitespace on a printed paper adds readability to the printed text by presenting the materials in a clean, uncluttered manner. Similarly, in speeches, pausing helps listeners to understand the speech better. Pausing also gives emphasis to the words before and after the pause. Imagine you seeing just one word on a plain white paper. Your attention is immediately drawn to that one word. Pause is the whitespace around spoken words.

Photo by Robinsonk26 on Pixabay

> The single biggest problem in communication is the illusion that it has taken place.
>
> **George Bernard Shaw**

SPEECH ASSIGNMENT

Grades 1-4

Speech Topic: **Book Report**
Speech Objective: **In this exercise, you will be presenting the report of a book that you read.**
Speech Length: **1-2 minutes**

Research and Critical Thinking

- Identify a fiction or a non-fiction book.
- Who is the author/illustrator?
- What is the book about?
- What is the story line, if it is a fiction book?
- What is the main idea, if it is a non-fiction book?
- What are some of the interesting things you've learned from this book?
- Would you recommend this book to others? Why?

Speech Structure

INTRODUCTION

- Tell the audience the objective of your speech, which is giving a book report.
- State the name of the book and the author.
- Give a one sentence summary of this book.

BODY

- Address some or all of the questions in the *Research and Critical Thinking* section.

CONCLUSION

- What is your recommendation?
- Thank the audience.

Photo by Susin Tipchai

SPEECH ASSIGNMENT

Grades 5-12

Speech Topic: **The purpose of education.**

Speech Objective: **Present your point of view on the purpose of education.**

Speech Length: **1-2 minutes**

Research and Critical Thinking

- What are the purposes of education?
- Have these purposes changed over time in history?
- Are we achieving what we wanted to achieve with our current education system?
- If not, why not?
- Would you suggest any changes to the current education system?

Speech Structure

INTRODUCTION

- Start with an interesting fact or story.

BODY

- Address some or all of the questions in the *Research and Critical Thinking* section.

CONCLUSION

- What is the main point that you want audience to remember?
- Thank the audience.

A NEW WORD TO USE IN YOUR SPEECH

inflection

Meaning: A change in pitch, tone, or loudness of the voice.

Example: Playing the part of Abraham Lincoln, the actor's inflection was perfect.

11

HOW TO PRESENT THE SPEECH

Walk to the stage with **confident steps.**

Keep a **power pose** and control unnecessary body movements.

Use **hand gestures** to express your ideas. Keep your hands in the **power circle**.

Keep **eye contact** with the audience.

Speak up, with pauses, and variation in your tone and pace.

Speak with **pauses**.

Control **mannerisms**, the "ahs" and "ums"

Show command knowledge on the topic

KEYNOTE SPEECH ASSIGNMENT

- Select a topic.
- Prepare a thesis statement.
- Create a brain dump.
- Identify the main points.
- Find some stories and examples.
- Write the first paragraph.
- Write the rest of the speech.
- Develop the introduction and conclusion.
- Edit the speech for flow and time.
- Review the speech with the instructor.

QUESTIONS AND EXERCISES

1 What does pace variation do in a speech?

2 Why is pausing an important?

3 Try telling a story with variation in pace, tone, and pitch.

SPEECH OUTLINE

Speech Title:

Through Line: Write the main idea of your speech in one or two sentences.

Introduction: Present your topic in an interesting way to hook the audience.

Body - Point 1: The idea, data, and examples.

Body - Point 2: The idea, data, and examples.

Conclusion: The main point that you want your audience to remember.

Mannerisms

Unnecessary sound fillers are a distraction in communication.

LESSON OBJECTIVES

- Learn to identify mannerisms.
- Practice to control mannerisms.
- Prepare, practice, and deliver your speeches.

Photo by Nikolay Georgiev

PRINCIPLES

12.1. What is mannerism?

Mannerisms in speech such as "ahs" and "ums" are developed over time and stuck in many people's speech pattern as a habit. Breaking such habits will take some time and effort. Sometimes, these mannerisms can come from nervousness and not nec-

essarily from habits. In such cases, once you are able to control your stage fright, the mannerisms will disappear.

There are other words also people use as a filler to fill any white space in their speech, such as the word "like" and "and". Remember from last lesson that whitespace is an

important part of your speech. So, don't try to fill all your white space with filler sounds.

Mannerisms do have a distracting effect on your audience. It dilutes the impact or effectiveness of your speech by the addition of these unnecessary word fillers.

Photo by Manan Chhabra

> You cannot truly listen to anyone and do anything else at the same time.
>
> **Scott Peck**

SPEECH ASSIGNMENT

Grades 1-4

Speech Topic: **Science Experiment**

Speech Objective: **In this exercise, you will be explaining or demonstrating a science experiment. Explain the steps of a science experiment, demonstrate it, and teach the scientific principles behind the experiment.**

Speech Length: **1-2 minutes**

Research and Critical Thinking

- Select an experiment, which will not make a mess in the classroom if you demonstrate it. There are experiments related to rainbow color wheel, gravity, simple machines, etc., that you can choose from.
- What materials do you need to perform this experiment?
- Can you do the experiment in 1-2 minutes?
- Do you need someone from the audience to assist you when you do the experiment?
- What is the science behind the results you get?
- Try the experiment at home and practice it before coming to the class.

Speech Structure

- Introduction
  - Tell the audience what the experiment is and where they can see the principles of this experiment in their day-to-day life.
- Body
  - Demonstrate the experiment and explain the steps.
  - If you are not demonstrating, explain the steps of the experiment in a detailed manner.
  - Explain the results of the experiment.
  - Explain the science behind the experiment
- Conclusion
  - Ask the students, if they have any questions.

Photo by Michal Jarmoluk

SPEECH ASSIGNMENT

Grades 5-12

Keynote Speech

- Keynote speech length is 3 minutes minimum and 5 minutes maximum.

- Date: _____

- Title: _____
  _____

- How would you like to be introduced: _____
  _____
  _____
  _____
  _____
  _____

- Thesis Statement: _____
  _____
  _____
  _____
  _____
  _____
  _____
  _____

Keynote Speech Evaluation		
Factor	**Evaluation**	**Total Score**
Appearance, Professionalism		10
Eye Contact, Facial Expressions		10
Posture, Gestures		10
Volume, Modulation, Pausing		10
Introduction - Effectiveness		15
Body - Content, Organization		15
Conclusion		15
Examples, Stories, Visual Aids		15
Time Limit		Y/N
Total		100

QUESTIONS AND EXERCISES

1   What are mannerisms?

2   Why do people put in filler sounds in their speech?

3   What are some of the ways to control mannerisms?

KEYNOTE SPEECH OUTLINE

Speech Title:

Through Line: Write the main idea of your speech in one or two sentences.

Introduction: Present your topic in an interesting way to hook the audience.

Body - Point 1: The idea, data, and examples.

Body - Point 2: The idea, data, and examples.

Conclusion: The main point that you want your audience to remember.

Listen with curiosity. Speak with honesty. Act with integrity. The greatest problem with communication is we don't listen to understand. We listen to reply. When we listen with curiosity, we don't listen with the intent to reply. We listen for what's behind the words.

Roy T. Bennett

Photo by Jon Tyson

Public Speaking Training Materials Available From Geo Publishers

To order any of the following titles, please send an email to geopublishers.usa@gmail.com.

Impromptu Speech Topic Cards - Beginner (36 topic cards)
High quality glossy cards with case   **$14.95**

Impromptu Speech Topic Cards - Intermediate (56 topic cards)
High quality glossy cards with case   **$18.95**

Impromptu Speech Topic Cards - Advanced (56 topic cards)
High quality glossy cards with case   **$18.95**

Impromptu Speech Topic Cards - Master (56 topic cards)
High quality glossy cards with case   **$18.95**

Motivational Quote Cards (56 cards)
High quality glossy cards with case   **$18.95**

Speak Right Up: Public Speaking Instructor's Guide
52 Weekly Lessons For Your Public Speaking Students   **$14.95**